R S
A B

THIS BOOK BELONGS TO

Daisy. xmas 2002

This edition published by HarperCollins Publishers Ltd 1999 for Silverdale Books
An imprint of Bookmart Ltd
Registered Number 2372865
Trading as Bookmart Limited
Desford Rd, Enderby, Leicester, LE9 5AD
First published 1964 by Sampson Lowe

ISBN 0 26 167257-6
Printed and bound in Italy

NODDY AND THE AEROPLANE

BY Enid Blyton

CONTENTS

1. Noddy Gives Tubby a Job
2. Tubby Bear Works Very Hard
3. Whatever is Wrong with the Car?
4. Bad Little Tubby Bear!
5. A Wonderful Surprise for Noddy!
6. Noddy Has Learned to Fly!
7. Tubby is Rather Silly
8. Noddy and the Aeroplane

"AN AEROPLANE THAT I CAN FLY MYSELF!"
SHOUTED NODDY

1. NODDY GIVES TUBBY A JOB

ONE day Noddy came home quite tired out. It had been a very busy day!

"I feel too tired even to clean you, little car," he said. "And you're very, *very* dirty, because it's such muddy weather."

"Parp-parp," said the car, in a little voice. It didn't like being dirty.

"I feel too tired even to sing a song," said Noddy, getting out of the car. "And I *had* thought of a very nice little coming-home song. It began like this: 'How nice it is to be home for tea, in a dear little house that is just for me, and . . .' "

"Noddy! Hallo, Noddy!" called a voice from over the fence. "Did you have a good day? Ooooh, isn't your car dirty?"

"Oh, hallo, little Tubby Bear," said Noddy, opening his garage doors. "How much trouble have you caused today? I hear you've been very naughty lately. It's about time you did something good for a change."

"I'd like to, Noddy," said Tubby, climbing over the fence. "I'd like to very much. Are you tired? Can I do something for *you?* I really *do* want to be good. I'm tired of being naughty."

"You're tired of being punished, you mean," said Noddy. "Now, if I could only *trust* you to be good, I'd ask you to clean my dirty little car. I feel just too tired to get out my bucket and my cloths, and . . ."

"NODDY! I'll clean your car all over, I'll make it shine and gleam, I'll make it as good as new!" shouted Tubby, in excitement. "Oh, LET me clean it! I can pretend it is *my* car. I'll get every speck of dirt off it, I'll . . ."

"All right, all right, don't shout," said Noddy, putting his hands over his ears. "You *could* clean my car well, I'm sure, but I just don't trust you. You'd do something silly – like take the hooter off and not put it back again — or take the wheels off and let them roll away down the road. I know you, Tubby. You may be small but you can make Very Big Mistakes."

"Please, PLEASE, dear Noddy, let me clean your car," begged Tubby. "You're always telling me to be good, and so are my father and mother, and now, when I want to be, you won't let me."

"Oh well—*clean* the car then!" said Noddy. "I'm too tired to stand here talking to you. There are the cloths, look—and remember you've got to wash them out when you've finished, and hang them up to dry on my line. And don't forget to put the lid on the polish tin—and don't DARE to try and drive the car, or I'll—I'll—well, I really don't know *what* I'll do! Throw you into the pond, I think."

"Oh, Noddy! Thank you!" said little Tubby Bear, feeling so joyful that he just had to fling his arms round Noddy. Down went

Noddy on the ground with a bump!

And at the very same moment who should come in at the gate but the Bumpy-Dog, leaping up and down as usual, and barking with delight to see Noddy on the ground. He thought that Noddy and Tubby were having a game, and he flung himself on poor Noddy and licked him all over his face.

"Bumpy-Dog! STOP it!" shouted Noddy. "When I want my face washed, I'll wash it myself. Pull him off me, Tubby Bear, and don't stand there laughing!"

"Bumpy! Come away from Noddy!" shouted Tubby. "Bumpy, you can help me to clean Noddy's car, if you like. BUMPY!"

Bumpy left Noddy and ran over to Tubby at once. Clean Noddy's car! What a very grand thing to do! He leapt happily up to lick Tubby's face, and down went Tubby, of course. Noddy got up and went indoors. Let Bumpy knock down Tubby Bear, let them both clean his car, let Tubby polish *Bumpy* if he liked! All Noddy wanted was to sit down with a nice hot cup of tea.

Tessie Bear was just passing by and saw Noddy going slowly indoors, looking half asleep. "You look tired, Noddy," she called to him. "I'll come and make tea for you. I've a ginger cake here. We'll have a nice tea together. Would you like that?"

"Oh *yes*, Tessie Bear!" said Noddy, pleased. "I feel just like eating some ginger cake. Oh, Tessie, I *am* pleased to see you. I feel very fond of bears at the moment. There's Tubby outside cleaning my dirty car for me—and you coming to tea—with a ginger cake, too!"

"I'm surprised you're letting that naughty little Tubby clean your car," said Tessie. "He might easily drive it away!"

"He can't," said Noddy. "The petrol tank is nearly empty. Oh, Tessie, let's have tea quickly. I'm so hungry."

And soon Noddy and Tessie were sitting down by the fire, eating toast made by

Noddy, and drinking tea made by Tessie, and enjoying the lovely ginger cake. But it wasn't peaceful for very long! Someone came and flung himself against the front door, and made Noddy jump so much that he spilt his tea.

"Woof!" said a voice.

"That's the Bumpy-Dog!" said Tessie. "Whatever is he doing? Bumpy-Dog, go home!"

Noddy yelled:

"Go home, Bumpy-Dog,
We're having our tea,
So please don't disturb
Little Tessie and me!"

But the Bumpy-Dog joined them just the same! He suddenly leapt in through the open window, and jumped up at Noddy, making him drop his toast. "Oh, BUMPY! Go away! Look at my nice toast—butter-side down, too. GO AWAY!"

2. TUBBY BEAR WORKS VERY HARD

THE Bumpy-Dog wouldn't go away, even when Tessie scolded him. He put himself into a corner, and whined tiny little whines, so that Noddy soon felt sorry for him. Then suddenly he leapt up and barked so loudly that he quite scared Tessie and Noddy. He ran to the door, growling, and pawed at it. Then he threw himself at it so that the door shook from top to bottom.

Noddy and Tessie were very surprised. "There must be someone outside—a burglar perhaps," said Tessie, in a scared little voice.

"HO! I'M not scared of burglars!" said Noddy, bravely, and he went to the door and flung it open. It was only little Tubby Bear! He had seen Tessie going into Noddy's house with the ginger cake and it had made him feel hungry for his tea!

"Please, Noddy, I've finished cleaning your car, and it looks very nice. I thought you'd like to come and see it," said Tubby. "Oooooh! What a LOVELY ginger cake!"

"You'd better have some, as you're being kind enough to clean Noddy's car," said Tessie Bear. "Come in."

"Wait a minute," said Noddy. "I'd rather like to go and see if Tubby has cleaned my car properly before we give him the ginger cake. It might be only half-done."

So out they went to look at the little car. My goodness me, Tubby had certainly worked hard! The little car shone and gleamed and glinted like new.

"Oh, TUBBY!" said Tessie Bear, surprised. "It really DOES look lovely! You certainly MUST come and have some cake!"

Little Tubby was very pleased. He was so hungry that he ate three huge slices, and Tessie had to stop him. "Just *look* at your tummy!" she said. "You'll burst in a minute. No more cake, Tubby."

"I don't want any reward for cleaning your

THE LITTLE CAR SHONE AND GLEAMED AND GLINTED LIKE NEW

car, Noddy," said Tubby. "But I would just like *one* thing."

"What's that?" asked Noddy.

"Let me drive it down the road and back," said Tubby.

"NO," said Noddy. "Anyway, it hasn't any petrol in the tank. NO, Tubby. I'm very grateful to you for cleaning my car so well and I'll give you a free ride whenever I see you—but you are NOT going to drive my car—no, not even push it out of the garage and let it run down the hill! You'd probably knock down half a dozen lamp-posts, and Mr Plod would be after me at once."

"All right," said Tubby, sadly. "Could you make up a little song about me instead? I'd like that very much."

"Oh, all right, Tubby," said Noddy. "Have another slice of cake, and I'll sing a song about you."

So while Tubby ate his fourth slice of cake. Noddy sang this little song:

"Oh, Tubby Bear, how good you are
To go and clean my little car.
You rubbed with all your might and main
To make it nice and clean again.
So dear kind Tubby Bear, please take
What's left of Tessie's ginger cake,
And eat it all, it won't last long . . .
And that's the finish of my song!"

"Oh, that's lovely, Noddy," said Tubby in delight. "I wish I could make up songs like you. How do you do it?"

"I don't know," said Noddy. "They just come into my head and I sing them. Well—you take the rest of the cake, and go now. I DO think you have cleaned the car well. I'll get some petrol for it in the morning, and then it will be quite as good as new."

Tubby Bear went off with the cake, looking very

proud and pleased.

Tessie Bear washed up the cups and saucers, then it was time for her to go. "The Bumpy-Dog hasn't had a proper run today so I'll give him a nice long walk before we go home," she said.

When he heard the word "walk" the Bumpy-Dog went quite mad, and leapt right over the tea-table. Tessie was really shocked at him.

"What *bad* manners, Bumpy!" she said. "I shan't take you out to tea again."

That made Bumpy put his tail down at once, and he went to sit by himself in a corner. "It's all right, Bumpy," said Noddy, patting him. "You didn't knock the teapot over, though your tail only *just* missed it! Go with Tessie Bear, now, and guard her well."

This made Bumpy feel much better, and his tail began to wag again. He went off with Tessie Bear, walking proudly in front of her, growling at any car that passed. Woof! Grrrrr! Don't you dare to splash Tessie Bear, cars!

Noddy went to his garage to look at his little car again. It was shining so very brightly.

"You really do look as good as new!" he said. "I'm sure Big-Ears will think I've bought a new car when he sees you. Oh—there *is* Big-Ears! Hey, Big-Ears, have you come to see me? Well, just look at my car!"

"Good gracious—is it *really* your car, Noddy?" said Big-Ears, surprised. "I've never seen it looking so bright and clean. Did *you* clean it?"

"No—little Tubby Bear did it for me," said Noddy, nodding his head up and down. "You wouldn't think such a bad little fellow could clean a car so well, would you? Won't everyone stare when I take it out tomorrow!"

"My word, yes!" said Big-Ears. "Come and call for me, in the morning, Noddy. We'll do my shopping and then have an ice-cream together. I'll feel proud to ride in a car as smart as yours is now! Don't forget—call for me tomorrow!"

3. WHATEVER IS WRONG WITH THE CAR?

NOW the next morning, when Noddy had washed up his breakfast things, and polished the bell on his hat, and made his bed, and baked a little pie in the oven, he went to the garage to get out his car. He sang a little song as he opened the doors:

"It's time for shopping, little car,
Goodness me, how clean you are!
Everyone will shout and say,
LOOK AT NODDY'S CAR TODAY!

"First of all, little car, we'll go down the hill to the garage, and have some petrol put into your tank," he said. "It must be quite empty after that long run we went on yesterday. Come along!"

He hopped into the car and pressed the starter, expecting to hear the car's usual happy noise. But instead of that it made a very curious sound indeed.

"Eekoff! Eekoff! Eekoff!"

And then it began to shake every time it said

"Eekoff", and Noddy bounced up and down as it shook.

"Car! Little car! What's wrong with you?" cried Noddy. "You keep jerking and jumping! What's happened?"

Noddy got out and looked under the car. It seemed all right. Then he tried it again. No—it just went "Eekoff, eekoff" and jumped again. Noddy sat down on a sack in the garage and wailed.

"Something's wrong with my car! It's making a funny noise and it won't go. Oh, *why* did I let Tubby Bear clean it for me yesterday? Why did I? Something's gone wrong with you, little car. Wait till I get hold of Tubby Bear—I'll shake him till all the buttons fly off his coat!"

"Eekoff!" said the little car, mournfully, and jerked up and down again.

Noddy ran into the garden and yelled at the top of his voice. "Tubby! Tubby! Where are you, you wicked little bear? What have you done to my car? It won't start. It just makes silly noises and jumps up and down. TUBBY! WHERE ARE YOU?"

Tubby Bear didn't answer. He had heard Noddy's angry voice and wasn't going to say a word. He crept upstairs and hid under his bed. Oh Tubby, what in the world have you done to Noddy's car? Oh yes—you cleaned it beautifully. But what ELSE did you do?

Noddy was so upset that he just didn't know what to do next. Should he fetch Big-Ears? Oh dear, he had promised to call for him that morning and take him shopping! It was difficult for Big-Ears to carry all his shopping home on his bicycle. Now he wouldn't be able to go.

"I *wish* I could find that naughty bear!" said Noddy. "Oh, my dear little car. I'll always clean you myself in future. Why do you keep on saying 'Eekoff, eekoff'? What does it mean?"

"Ee-koff," said the little car, with a sudden little jerk. Noddy waited and waited for little Tubby Bear to come out into the garden, but he didn't come. Noddy had just made up his mind to go and look for him, when he heard a very welcome sound.

It was the ringing of a bicycle bell!

"Big-Ears! Oh, Big-Ears, I *am* pleased to see you!" shouted Noddy, rushing out into the road. Yes—it was dear old Big-Ears, pedalling along on his bicycle, and ringing his bell loudly to let Noddy know he was there.

"Noddy! Why didn't you come in your car to take me shopping?" cried Big-Ears, jumping off his bicycle. "I waited and waited. Then I thought you must be ill, so I came to find out."

"Oh Big-Ears, something dreadful has happened to my car," wailed Noddy. Big-Ears looked at the car in surprise.

"But it looks simply beautiful!" he said. "I haven't seen it so bright and clean for a long time. What's wrong with it?"

"Well, look what happens when I press the starter," said Noddy, and he pressed.

"Eekoff!" said the car at once, and jerked up and down. "Eekoff! Eekoff! Eekoff!"

"There!" said Noddy. "It keeps on and on

doing that, and it won't go. I think it's gone mad."

"Good gracious!" said Big-Ears, most astonished. "No—it hasn't gone mad, poor little car. It's got something *you* sometimes get, Noddy."

"What has it got?" asked Noddy, surprised.

"It's got *hiccups!*" said Big-Ears. "That's all. Listen—there it goes again. 'Eekoff—eekoff'—that's its way of hiccupping. And that's why it jumps and jerks—you do, don't you, when you've got bad hiccups!"

"Oh Big-Ears! Has my little car *really* got hiccups?" said Noddy, in astonishment. "It's never, never had them before. I didn't even know that cars could hiccup. WHY has it got them? How can I stop them? What am I to do? Why has . . .?"

"Goodness! Stop asking so many questions!" said Big-Ears. "Let me see now—people get hiccups if they drink something fizzy too quickly—or if they . . ."

"But my car doesn't eat or drink, Big-Ears!" cried Noddy. "You know it doesn't. Is it ill? Is it in pain? Oh, what shall I do?"

"It isn't ill. It isn't in pain. How can you be so silly, Noddy?" said Big-Ears, sounding quite stern. "What have you put into its petrol-tank? Did you put in some different petrol—or have you poured something else into it?"

"No—no, of course not!" said Noddy. "I only give it petrol, and always the same sort. Oh, poor little car—there it goes, hiccupping again! Big-Ears, tell me what to do! We must make it better!"

"I think that little scamp of a Tubby has given the car something silly to drink!" said Big-Ears. "Something which has upset it badly."

"Eekoff!" said the little car, sadly, and jerked up and down again. Poor little car! What in the world could be done for it? It couldn't be driven. It couldn't stand still. It could only hiccup!

4. BAD LITTLE TUBBY BEAR!

"NODDY—we shall have to get Tubby here and ask him what he's done to the car," said Big-Ears. "He must have put something in the tank that's upset it—but what could it be?"

Noddy and Big-Ears looked all round the small garage. There were tins in one corner, and a box in another. There was a shelf with little boxes of nails and screws and odds and ends. And there was another shelf with little bottles on it.

"Nothing much here," said Big-Ears. Noddy suddenly looked puzzled and went over to the shelf where the little bottles stood.

"I don't remember these, Big-Ears," he said. "Oh—they're empty. What did they have in them?"

Big-Ears looked at them closely. "Ginger-beer!" he said. "GINGER-BEER! Noddy, have *you* been buying ginger-beer lately?"

"Good gracious, no," said Noddy. "I haven't

enough money for ginger-beer. Wherever did these bottles come from?"

"We'll soon find out!" said Big-Ears, and, with Noddy following close behind, he marched out of the garage and went to the Tubby Bears' front gate. He swung it open, and went up to the front door. RAT-A-TAT-TAT! How loudly he knocked!

Mrs Tubby Bear answered the door. "Oh, hallo Big-Ears!" she said, cheerfully. "How nice to see you! What do you want?"

"I'd like a word with little Tubby Bear, please," said Big-Ears. "But perhaps you could tell me something before I see him, Mrs Tubby. Have you bought any bottles of ginger-beer lately?"

"What an extraordinary question, Big-Ears!" said Mrs Tubby Bear, astonished. "Yes—yes, I bought quite a lot, because we all like ginger-beer."

"Have you noticed any bottles missing?" asked Big-Ears, in such a stern voice that Mrs Tubby looked quite frightened.

"Er—well, yes, we did miss quite a few," she said. "We thought that our naughty little Tubby must have taken them to drink, you know. They—er—well, they did disappear rather quickly. I was cross because I wanted to take the empty bottles back to the shop."

"Well, there are a whole lot in Noddy's garage," said Big-Ears. "Quite empty. Could I see Tubby, now, please?"

"Tubby! Tubby, where are you?" shouted Mrs Tubby Bear. But Tubby didn't reply. "I'll go and find him," said Big-Ears, firmly, and ran upstairs to Tubby's bedroom. There was no one to be seen, but Big-Ears caught sight of a small paw sticking out from under the bed. He pounced on it and dragged out a very frightened little Tubby Bear.

"Ha! And may I ask why you are hiding?" asked Big-Ears sternly, as Noddy and Mrs Tubby came into the room.

"No, you may not!" said Tubby, rudely. "Go away!"

Then Mrs Tubby

BIG-EARS CAUGHT SIGHT OF A SMALL PAW STICKING OUT

scolded him so furiously that naughty little Tubby began to cry. "What did you do with that ginger-beer?" she said. "Surely you didn't drink it all?"

"No, I didn't," said Tubby. "I cleaned Noddy's car for him, but he said I couldn't drive it because it had run out of petrol, so I went and got the bottles of ginger-beer and . . ."

"Tubby, you SURELY didn't pour ginger-beer into my little car's petrol tank!" wailed Noddy.

"I did," said Tubby. "I thought it would go all right on that. I thought it might like some ginger-beer for a change. But it wouldn't go. It—it . . ."

"Yes—we know what it did. It got hiccups," said Big-Ears, very sternly. "And now it won't go at all. It just stands there, hiccupping and jerking. And I expect it will take a long time to put right again. Poor little car! Tubby, you have been a *very* bad little bear and you deserve to be punished."

"He certainly does," said Mrs Tubby. She was very shocked to think of all that Tubby Bear had done. Tubby Bear

gave a howl and disappeared under the bed again.

"I only gave the car a drink!" he wailed. "Its tank was almost empty. It was THIRSTY! It *wanted* a drink!"

"Rubbish!" said Big-Ears. "You wanted to drive it away for a treat after you'd cleaned it—even though Noddy had told you not to. And now you've managed to spoil Noddy's car. It will have to go to the garage and be cleaned out properly, and Noddy won't be able to have it until it is better again!"

This made Tubby cry even more loudly.

"You must stay in your room until you say you are sorry," said his mother. "And you can empty your money-box to pay Noddy for all the damage you have caused! I never in my life heard of such a thing. Fancy trying to drive a car on *ginger-beer!*"

"Will my car be all right again soon, Big-Ears?" said Noddy, as they went downstairs. He was feeling as if he wanted to howl too, like naughty Tubby.

"Well—it will have to go for a good clean," said Big-Ears. "It looks to me as if Tubby has spilt ginger-beer over the engine as well as emptying it into the tank. It may take quite a long time. It would damage your car badly if you drove it before all the ginger-beer had gone."

"But, Big-Ears—what shall I do if I haven't a car?" said Noddy, with tears in his eyes. "I can't take people about. I can't earn any money. What shall I DO?"

"Cheer up, little Noddy, we'll think of something!" said Big-Ears. "You've plenty of friends, you know. We'll think of *something* you can do. Don't worry!"

5. A WONDERFUL SURPRISE FOR NODDY!

NODDY was very unhappy about his little car. It was taken down to the garage to be thoroughly cleaned and overhauled.

"They say it will take at least three weeks before I can have my car back," said Noddy mournfully. "Oh, that horrid, nasty, unkind, silly, stupid, careless Tubby!"

"Dear me—what a lot of words you know!" said Big-Ears. "Now just be patient, Noddy. I *think* I'll be able to get something rather exciting for you to use while your car is being mended. But you must just be PATIENT!"

So Noddy was very patient, even though whenever he saw his empty garage he felt sad and worried. And then something VERY exciting happened.

An aeroplane flew over Noddy's house. Then it flew round and round, lower and lower—and then it landed right in Noddy's garden! Think of that! An aeroplane in his garden! He was very surprised!

Noddy ran into the garden and the Tubby Bears ran out into their garden next door. What excitement there was!

Then, would you believe it? Who should jump out of the aeroplane but Big-Ears, followed by a very smart little pilot. Noddy rushed up to them.

"Big-Ears! What are you doing in an aeroplane? Where have you come from? Did you fly it—or did the pilot here fly it? Oh, Big-Ears, could I have a ride?"

"Now listen, Noddy," said Big-Ears, solemnly. "I have a very big surprise for you. Mr and Mrs Tubby Bear are so very sorry that little Tubby spoilt your car, that they have asked one of their cousins—this pilot here—to lend you his aeroplane till your car is all right again. We will teach you how to fly—it's quite easy, you know—and then you can use the plane to carry people's shopping and travel about till your own car is

better again."

"Big-Ears! I can't believe it! An aeroplane to ride in—one that I can fly myself!" Noddy shouted at the top of his voice, he was so excited and pleased. "Let me get in! Oh, let me get in!"

"Well, you can *certainly* get in," said the jolly-looking pilot, who had been shaking hands with his cousins, the Tubby Bears. "But you mustn't fly it till I'm quite certain you know how."

"*I* want to get in! *I* want to fly it!" shouted little Tubby Bear in great excitement. He tried to push Noddy away. But Mr Tubby Bear took hold of him and held him tightly under his arm. "Any more trouble from you, little Tubby, and you'll end up in bed for a week!" he said. "On no account are you even to go *near* that plane!"

He carried poor Tubby, kicking and struggling, into the house. Noddy couldn't help feeling sorry for Tubby, but he was so excited that he didn't feel sorry for long. An aeroplane for him to fly! Oh, what would everyone say? What would Tessie Bear think—and the Bumpy-Dog—when they saw him sailing over the rooftops? It was the most exciting moment in Noddy's life!

"Get in," said the pilot. "I'll show you how to fly. It's easier than driving a car. You don't have to bother about corners or lamp-posts or keeping to the left, or anything like that. You just fly!"

Well, the pilot was right. It *was* easier than driving a car. And before very long, Noddy was flying that little aeroplane by himself! Oh, what joy! What excitement! Surely he must be dreaming!

No, you're not dreaming, Noddy! You are flying a dear little aeroplane all by yourself, with Big-Ears and the pilot sitting close by to make sure you don't make a mistake. Clever little Noddy! Even the pilot says he has never seen anyone learn to fly so quickly!

Now—down to the ground—look, Noddy, this is how you do it. Gently, now, gently—watch that dial—it tells you how near the ground you are—you don't need to keep leaning out. Gently, now—you're nearly there!

BUMP! That was rather too big a bump, Noddy, but, after all, it was your very first landing!

"Well done!" said Big-Ears and the pilot together. "Splendid, Noddy!"

"Oh, it was WONDERFUL!" cried Noddy, his face all smiles. "Can I really use it until my car's mended? Oh, I shall have such fun! I'll fly over people's roofs and shout down their chimneys—I'll fly round Mr Plod's head and give him such a scare! I'll . . ."

"Oh well—if that's the sort of thing you want to do, I'll ask the pilot to take it away again," said Big-Ears, in such a cross voice that Noddy felt quite alarmed.

"Oh, Big-Ears—I'm only joking!" said Noddy.

"I'll use the aeroplane like I do my car, to carry parcels and give people lifts. And I'll use it to fetch my shopping and visit people who live far away. Oh, WON'T they be surprised when I land in their back gardens! I'll have to look out for washing-lines, though, won't I?"

"You certainly will," said Big-Ears. "Now let me get out of this seat, Noddy. I'm too fat for such a small space. I feel quite cramped. Well, thank you very much, pilot. I think I can teach Noddy anything else he needs to know about flying. Don't worry, he'll take good care of your plane!"

They said goodbye to the pilot, and soon were up in the air again with Big-Ears showing Noddy lots of different ways to fly—round and round – up and down – fast or slow.

"Let's loop the loop!" said Noddy, thrilled. "I'll turn the aeroplane right over and we'll see everything upside down!"

"No, we will NOT," said Big-Ears, firmly. "I don't want to find myself falling through the air and landing on somebody's chimney. Now let me help you to land in your own garden. It's rather a small place to land in, and we don't want to spoil your flowers. Now—gently does it!"

And to the enormous astonishment of everyone in Noddy's street, the aeroplane landed neatly in the very middle of Noddy's back garden! What a to-do there was! Mr Plod came rushing up, shouting.

"Here, what's all this? Where did you get that aeroplane, Noddy? Who told you you could land it here? How do you know how to fly it?"

"I'll take you for a ride, Mr Plod!" cried Noddy. But Mr Plod wouldn't go.

"You've no right to fly that aeroplane without a proper permit!" he said. "Come along to the police station with me, Noddy—and you too, Big-Ears. We'll have to see about this aeroplane. We can't have everyone flying about all over the town. I've never heard of such a thing in all my life!"

6. NODDY HAS LEARNED TO FLY!

NODDY and Big-Ears, followed by quite a number of other people, and a very excited Bumpy-Dog, went along to the police station. Mr Plod listened to the sad story of Noddy's car being filled with ginger-beer by naughty little Tubby. Tubby, who had come to the police station too, slipped off very quietly. He was afraid he might be scolded by Mr Plod!

"Now you listen to me, Mr Plod!" said Big-Ears. "Mr and Mrs Tubby Bear got this aeroplane for Noddy and they want him to use it until his car's mended. It's their way of making up for all the trouble Tubby's caused. So just be sensible and kind and give Noddy permission to use it to take people about until his car's ready again."

"Yes. Tell him he can use it!" shouted everyone who was listening. "Hurrah for little Noddy!"

"Oh, very well," said Mr Plod. "But if you so much as touch a chimney-pot, Noddy, or land where you shouldn't, I'll be after you, and I'll lock

up both you *and* your aeroplane!"

"You do sound cross, Mr Plod," said Noddy. "Are you sure you won't come for a ride in the plane with me? You'll feel better then."

But Mr Plod wouldn't and Noddy and Big-Ears went out of the police station. "He's a horrid old grumpy!" said Noddy. "I've a good mind to knock his chimney right off his roof—bang, bang!"

"Now don't talk like that, Noddy, or you won't keep your aeroplane for long!" said Big-Ears. "I'll take you up for one more lesson, then you'll be able to fly without me."

"Oooh—I could have flown without you all along!" boasted Noddy.

"If you talk like that, you'll get swollen-headed and make the aeroplane overbalance!" said Big-Ears. "Swollen heads are very bad in aeroplanes. Now hurry along!"

Well, soon Noddy could fly the aeroplane just as well as he could drive his car. The only trouble was so many birds kept coming to see the plane that they kept getting

in Noddy's way. He decided to fly down to the garage and landed beautifully just where his car was being mended. There it was, in a shed, half cleaned out already!

"Hallo—your car's not ready yet," said the garage-man in surprise. "Hey—don't take its hooter!"

"I'll just borrow it for a while. I'm flying an aeroplane at the moment," said Noddy, proudly, "and the birds keep getting in my way. So I thought I'd get my hooter to warn them to move."

Off he went with his hooter, and fixed it to the side of the aeroplane. Now the birds would be safe. Parp-parp-parp! How surprised they were to hear a car's hooter in the sky!

It wasn't very long before Noddy was almost as good at flying the aeroplane as Big-Ears and the instructor.

"I think we'll go back to my house for dinner," said Big-Ears. "Let me fly the plane now, Noddy. There's a very nice hollyhock out in

THE BIRDS WERE SURPRISED TO HEAR A
CAR'S HOOTER IN THE SKY!

my garden — and my washing is on the line, too. I don't want it spoilt — or the holly-hock knocked down."

So Noddy and Big-Ears changed places, and they rose into the air once more, and flew off over the woods. When Big-Ears saw the roof of his Toadstool House, he began to go down and down—and then landed with a bit of a bump on the grass just beside the washing-line.

Noddy leapt out. He was so pleased with everything that had happened that day, that he couldn't help dancing all over the little garden, singing at the top of his voice!

"Oh, would you believe it, I've learnt to fly!
Up in the air I go, oh so high!
Maybe I'll visit the moon and the sun,
Or land on a star—oh, that *would* be fun!
I might find a rainbow, a-glittering bright,
And bring it back—what a wonderful sight!
Oh, would you believe it, I've learnt to fly!
Up in the air I go, oh so high!"

"Well, that's a fine little song about flying, Noddy," said Big-Ears, unpegging the clothes from his line. "Now I'll just go and get some ham from my larder while you lay the table for me. We'll have a nice little dinner together."

They soon had their dinner and talked and talked about what Noddy was going to do with the plane. Noddy said he was going to fly over to Rocking-Horse Town, and have a ride on the horses, and go to Bouncing-Ball Village and bring some nice balls back with him, and take Tessie Bear to Teddy-Bear Town to visit her Grandma, and . . .

"Stop, Noddy! You're making my ears ache!" said Big-Ears at last. "Where are you going to get the money to buy petrol for all these wonderful journeys?"

"Ooooh—I hadn't thought of that!" said Noddy. "Dear me, yes, I MUST earn some money, or I won't have anything to eat. Do you think I could take people shopping in my plane? I'd be very careful with their parcels—and I'm sure I could land neatly just beside any shop."

"Well, we'll put up a notice in the post office about you and your aeroplane," said Big-Ears. "Do you think you could land your plane very carefully in the post-office yard? You'll have to mind the sacks of letters waiting there to be collected. And watch out for the post-office cat too—she'll be sitting near the sacks!"

Noddy was soon in his plane, with Big-Ears beside him. He flew slowly down into the post-office yard, feeling very excited. Gently, Noddy, carefully now—mind that pile of sacks! That's right! Bumpety-bump. That was your wheels touching the ground. Now you're safely down!

So he was—and everyone came rushing out of the post office to see the little plane—postmen, dolls, teddy bears, a clockwork mouse and lots of other toys. How excited they all were!

7. TUBBY IS RATHER SILLY

"WELL that wasn't a bad landing, Noddy," said Big-Ears. "A *bit* of a bump, but not much. Hey, everyone, get away! You can't get into the plane, there isn't room!"

Well, it was lucky that Mr Plod came rushing up just then, or the little plane would have been swamped with excited people.

"Fly off!" he ordered. "All right, Big-Ears, you can get out if you want to. Noddy, you must take the plane away. You can't park aeroplanes in the post-office yard."

So Big-Ears ran into the post office to put up a notice about Noddy doing everyone's shopping as usual but using the plane instead of his car, and Noddy pressed the switch that made the aeroplane rise into the air. But, oh dear, he didn't know that naughty little Tubby Bear was holding on to the end of one of the wings!

There he was, swinging by his paws, looking as

frightened as can be. Everyone yelled at Noddy, "COME DOWN! COME DOWN! Tubby Bear's hanging on to the plane!"

But the plane's engine was making such a noise that Noddy couldn't hear. He flew off with poor little Tubby clinging on with all his might, yelling and crying.

"What a silly little Tubby he is!" said Big-Ears. "Fancy catching hold of the plane just as it was going up!"

"Save him, oh please save my little Tubby!" wept poor Mrs Tubby Bear. "Ask that big crow over there to fly up and tell Noddy that Tubby's hanging on."

Well, the crow was quite willing to warn Noddy and flew up into the air at once. But as soon as it came near the plane, Noddy shouted at it. "Get away, crow!" he said. "Can't you see my plane? It will fly into you. Go away!"

The crow did its best to land on the plane, but then Noddy tooted his hooter loudly. "PARP-PARP-PARP!"

The crow had such a shock when it heard a car's hooter up in the sky that it flew away at once. Whatever next? Cars hooting in the sky! Really, Mr Plod would have to do something about it! The crow felt very worried indeed.

The little aeroplane didn't like Tubby Bear hanging on to it. It made it feel lop-sided. So it swooped down low over the nice big pond in Mr Jumbo's garden, and then shot up again quickly. Poor Tubby was thrown off, and down he went into the pond with a most terrific SPLASH! The aeroplane rose up into the air, and roared with its big voice.

"RRR-RRR-RRR-RRR!
Listen, you people down there, while I sing,
It's silly to hang on an aeroplane wing.
If you're REALLY wanting an aeroplane ride,
It's safer, much safer, to travel inside!
RRR-RRR-RRRRRRRR!"

Mr Jumbo was sitting quietly reading by the pond, and the big splash made by Tubby soaked him from head to foot. He leapt up very crossly. "What do you mean, Tubby, by jumping out of an aeroplane into my pond and wetting me like this?" he roared—and poor little Tubby ran for his life! Oh dear, oh dear, whatever made him think that it would be fun to go up with an aeroplane?

"I never will again, never, never!" he wept, as he trotted home, a very wet and miserable little bear. "I'll never be naughty again, either. Nasty things happen when I'm naughty. Oh dear—I KNOW I'm going to be scolded for getting my clothes all wet!"

Noddy had heard the splash and seen what had happened. He was sorry for Tubby, but he couldn't help laughing. What a little silly!

"Well—he won't need a bath tonight, after his swim in the pond," thought Noddy. He leaned out and saw Big-Ears signalling to him from the ground. He flew down carefully and landed with the very smallest bump just beside Big-Ears.

"What's happened to Tubby Bear?" said Big-Ears. "He was hanging on to your plane?"

"He landed in Mr Jumbo's

TUBBY WENT INTO THE POND WITH A MOST TERRIFIC SPLASH

pond!" said Noddy. "He's quite safe, but rather wet! Where shall we go now?"

"Well, I heard that Miss Monkey wants her suitcase taken to the station," said Big-Ears. "She was afraid she'd miss the train so she's left her case in the garden and gone on ahead. You can fly down and pick it up, and take it straight to her. Do you think you can land in her back garden—or shall I?"

"Big-Ears, I'm a very good pilot already!" said Noddy, proudly, and they set off in the air again. Noddy flew over Miss Monkey's house, and then went slowly down into the garden. It was a pity he landed right on top of Miss Monkey's suitcase, and dented it—but still, as Big-Ears said, there wasn't much damage—only a scratch or two. They put the case in the back of the plane and set off for the station.

The train was ready to leave. Miss Monkey waved her umbrella madly at their plane. "Where's my suitcase? The train's just going!"

Noddy was in such a fluster that he didn't think what he was doing. He gave the case a shove and it fell straight out of the plane. Down, down, down—BUMP! Where had it landed?

"Well — what a bit of luck!" said Big-Ears, with a chuckle. "It's landed safely in the coal-wagon — on top of the coal, look! The engine driver looks very surprised indeed. I expect it made him jump, seeing a case coming out of the air like that! You'll have to tell Miss Monkey that she owes you a shilling for delivering her suitcase so cleverly!"

8. NODDY AND THE AEROPLANE

WELL, Noddy had a wonderful time that week delivering all kinds of things in his aeroplane, and carrying people to and fro from the station, or taking them to other towns.

It was all very exciting. And he earned quite a lot of money too. But he did miss his little car. He didn't like to think of the empty garage at night. He wondered how the car was getting on. Was the tank clean yet? Had all the ginger-beer come out? Would the engine go all right now—or would there be something so wrong with it that it would never go properly again?

Noddy kept going to the garage to ask about his car, but always the answer was the same. "Sorry—it's not right yet. Call again."

The aeroplane was great fun—but it wasn't like his own dear little car. And the aeroplane sometimes got Noddy into trouble, too.

Once it landed right in the very middle of Miss Harriet Kitten's roses, and Noddy had to pay her for each broken bush. Another time, it landed so that one of its wings knocked off Bert Monkey's hat, which rolled straight into the pond. He was very cross.

"Why don't you tell that plane to look where it's going?" said Bert, angrily. "Now I can't wear my hat, and the cold wind will give me an earache. Well—if I have to call the doctor, *you'll* pay the bill. Unless you'd like to take me up in your plane for a ride instead?"

"No, I wouldn't," said Noddy. "I don't trust that silly tail of yours! It would come creeping round my arm and try to steer the aeroplane—then we'd probably crash! I think I *won't* take you for a ride, Bert Monkey!"

Then a dreadful thing happened. Noddy was just dropping slowly down to the road to land Mr Noah by the Ark, when someone came rushing by on a bicycle. Noddy didn't see him coming, and, oh dear, the person was knocked

off his bicycle, and his hat rolled away into the gutter.

Noddy landed and leapt out of the plane to help. Oh dear, oh dear, oh dear—Noddy had bumped into Mr Plod! His bicycle lay beside him, and his helmet was bowling merrily down the street.

"I'm sorry, I'm sorry, I'm sorry!" said Noddy, his head nodding madly. "I didn't mean it. I didn't, did I, Mr Noah? Oh dear, Mr Plod, don't be angry!"

But Mr Plod *was* angry. He hustled Mr Noah into the Ark, and then he called to Noddy.

"What do you mean by that dangerous bit of flying? You did it on purpose! You saw me on my bicycle, and you knocked me off. Fetch my helmet at once before it rolls miles away. And you can take that aeroplane straight back to its owner, or else I'll put you in prison. I never heard of such a thing in all my life—and just look at my helmet, rolling into that puddle! Just you wait, Noddy —JUST YOU WAIT!"

But Noddy didn't wait, he was so very frightened. He ran off as fast as he could to Big-

Ears' Toadstool House, leaving the aeroplane behind. He'd never fly it again! Oh dear, WHY did it have to fly down on Mr Plod? And where was Big-Ears? Wasn't he at home? Noddy did want him so. He was trying not to cry now. Would he be taken to prison for knocking over Mr Plod? Oh—oh—OH!

The last "OH" was a very big, sad one. Big-Ears wasn't at home! Where was he then? "BIG-EARS!" shouted Noddy. "I'M IN TROUBLE! I WANT YOU, DEAR BIG-EARS!"

He sat down at last to listen for Big-Ears' bicycle bell. He must have gone shopping. Well, he'd soon be back. "I'll listen for the tinkle-tinkle of his bell," thought Noddy, and he sat listening for so long that he almost fell asleep.

Then suddenly Noddy heard a noise that made him leap to his feet. It wasn't the tinkle of a bicycle bell. No—it wasn't that. It was—yes, it really WAS a noise that sounded like "PARP-PARP-PARP!"

"It's my *car!* I know it is! My own little car. Oh, it is, it is!" cried Noddy, and ran down the path.

And there, coming up to the Toadstool House, was Big-Ears—and he was driving Noddy's car!

Noddy ran to meet them, and the car was so pleased and excited that it jigged up and down saying "parpparpparp" without stopping. Big-Ears got out and Noddy leapt into the driver's seat and began to sing a very loud song indeed.

"Oh, here's my litle car again,
Hallo, little car!
You're feeling very well, it's plain,
How full of joy you are!
You're jigging about like anything,
Parp-parping as you go,
I feel as happy as a king,
Dear little car, hallo!"

Big-Ears stood beside him, laughing. When Noddy had finished, he clapped him on the back.

"A very nice little song, Noddy!" he said. "I *thought* you'd sing for joy when I brought back your car."

"I'm so glad to see it, Big-Ears!" cried Noddy. "Did you know that I knocked Mr Plod off his bicycle? Oh dear, you should have seen his helmet bowling down the street into a puddle, you really should!"

"I heard all about it," said Big-Ears. "I rode up on my bicycle and was most surprised to see your aeroplane all by itself with nobody in it—and Mr Plod raging round, holding his muddy helmet in his hand."

"Oh dear," said Noddy, looking rather scared. "Was he *very* angry?"

"Well he told me that he wasn't going to let you use the aeroplane again," said Big-Ears. "So I took off the hooter and went with it to the garage. Then I found that the car was ready to go back to you. So I drove it back straight away—and here it is—and here you are, in it! What about singing another of your nice little songs, as a payment for all I've done?"

"Oh, I will, I will!" cried Noddy, bouncing up and down in his car. "Oh, you are wonderful, Big-Ears, the best friend in all the world! Oh, I'm SO happy! Listen to my song, Big-Ears—it's all about you!"

And Noddy sang this song. Big-Ears liked it

the best of all Noddy's songs, and I'm not surprised, are you?

"Oh, dear old Big-Ears,
I do love you so!
You're my very good friend,
The best that I know!
I love your white whiskers,
I love your red hat,
I love your big smile,
And I do love your cat!
I love you to visit me,
Trundling along
On your old bicycle,
Singing your song.
Oh, DEAR old Big-Ears,
I DO love you so!
You're my very good friend,
The best that I know!"